ALSO BY A.P. FUCHS

FICTION

A Stranger Dead
A Red Dark Night
April (writing as Peter Fox)
Magic Man (deluxe chapbook)
The Way of the Fog (The Ark of Light Vol. 1)
Devil's Playground (written with Keith Gouveia)

NON-FICTION

Book Marketing
for the Financially-challenged Author

POETRY

The Hand I've Been Dealt
Haunted Melodies and Other Dark Poems

Go to
www.apfuchs.com

still about a girl

by

A.P. Fuchs

COSCOM ENTERTAINMENT
WINNIPEG

COSCOM ENTERTAINMENT
Suite 2, 317 Edison Avenue
Winnipeg, MB R2G 0L9

This book, though poetry, is a work of fiction. Names, characters, places and events either are products of the author's imagination or are used fictitiously. Any resemblance to actual events or persons living or dead is purely coincidental.

ISBN 1-897217-21-8

STILL ABOUT A GIRL
Copyright © 2005 by Adam P. Fuchs. All rights reserved, including the right to reproduce in whole or in part in any form.

PUBLISHED BY COSCOM ENTERTAINMENT
www.coscomentertainment.com

Cover art and design by A.P. Fuchs
Text set in Garamond
Printed and bound in the USA

Library and Archives Canada Cataloguing in Publication

Fuchs, A. P. (Adam Peter), 1980-
    Still about a girl / A. P. Fuchs.

Poems.
ISBN 1-897217-21-8

    I. Title.

PS8611.U34S75 2005   C811'.6   C2005-905171-X

This is for those who loved and lost, but still hang onto the memory of what it was like to be with the one who made their life complete.

still about a girl

Contents

I think I'm almost there	15
echoes	16
cigarettes and words…gone	18
hidden song	19
no title	20
held	21
just once in awhile	22
even then	23
lest you forget	24
it is still there	25
miss you	27
your words of color make me think of you	28
things change	30
she needs to be free…but He is here	31
you held me, we sang	32
it's okay	33
Mr. Fuchs's time unkempt	34
her fire within	36
stream (16)	37
long time	38
not done	39
happy anniversary	40
simply stated	41
never know	42
stream (9)	43
day to night	44
saturday	45
when she sleeps	47
coffee, cigarettes, 2AM	49
and if there's time	51
can't find a way	53
a love poem	55
never what she needed me to be	57
echo's shoulder	58

stream (5)	59
'til you came along my way	60
my princess	62
then…is better now	63
the day we were supposed to meet	64
Sandy smiles	66
giving in	67
a past origin	68
is it me?	69
you are yesterday	70
Fallon's song	71
falling away	73
something I had to say	74
she keeps me warm	75
and more	76
angels are on earth	77
so carefully there	78
don't remind me	79
drawn in, thrown out	80
there is no fate	81
stream (3)	83
over	84
her cheek rests in my hand	85
way back when (one more time)	86
play, night, love	87
can't forget	88
if you were near (I'm at a loss)	90
stream (17)	92
the edge	93
random (though sane)	94
poem undone	96
you're not alone	97
up to this place	98
you walked away	100
Sandy, what if?	102
stream (8)	103
all these things (just for you)	104

why must we suffer alone 106
Sandy 107
she gets it, you get it…I suppose I do, too 109

I think I'm almost there...

I think I'm almost there, almost at the bottom. But I don't think there is a bottom and yet, at the same time, there's sure as hell nothing up here, either. I'm only falling. Falling and sinking into this murk of self-deception yet self-appreciation all the same. I actually appreciate my loss and how it's making me fall, sink, drown.

Sometimes, my feet hit the ever-elusive bottom, only for the tacky slime beneath my feet to give way, causing me to be pulled into the dark and the cesspool of damaged emotion. Nothing but haunted love under promises of what is supposed to be the end of my turmoil. The end of the pain you inflict.

It's always nice when someone throws me a line, a ring of life in a grand effort to draw me back to the surface. One time, I had almost made it to the top. Only mere inches from the surface of the salty, cloudy depth. Through the poisoned haze, my stinging eyes caught the glimmers of daylight and the smile of someone with red hair. But she had let go of the rope because I also reached for someone else who had come along to try and pull me out. In the end...I was drowning again.

But as of this writing, I think I'm almost there, all the more immersed in sewage, somewhere close to the bottom. I think it's down there, six feet away. If only I can finally hit the bottom, maybe then I could breathe, and I wouldn't have to keep dying in you anymore.

echoes

I don't know what he said to you
I know some, not all
you told me

I was angry at first
so, so, so long ago
but no more
not for a while
there has been nothing but kind thoughts
kind words
kind years, going by
missing you

I'm not crazy like he would have you believe
I'm not crazy like you would have yourself believe
I'm not crazy

you may never believe me when I say,
"I don't know what you're talking about,"
or, "I never said that,"
and that's okay...not really
but I'll live

it's almost amusing how he brought up the past
brought up the verbalized pain that I shared with him secretly
and I'm not surprised he used his hate toward me
to turn you toward me
me toward you

ask someone else sometime
ask them how I feel about you
what I've always felt
even as I dated another

still about a girl

I promised I'd love you forever
and I do
not to stay true to my words
only to how things are, and will be

I asked for you
He gave
I lost you

I'm not crazy
no one sees that

I am alone

cigarettes and words...gone

drawing on cigarettes
feeling the rain beat down inside
utter apathy and helplessness
taking hold

I'm where I never thought I'd be:
starless, wasting, missing you
more and more and more
just more

damn...

someone's here now as I write this
I've lost my train of thought
train of feeling
I don't care

still about a girl

hidden song

imagine the smiles of hidden feelings
scared to reveal themselves in an array of stars
each thought independent of one another
each heart a child's own

there is a story about a poet no older than me
who drew her courage from a seagull's eyes
a girl without fingers, paper or ink
her mind the journal of her dreams

she talked to the squirrels of Fetterman Park
the trees a whisper of shade
her journals getting fuller after every visit
the leaves starting to lose their green

she makes a guitar out of fish-string and branches
and tells about the diary in her head
nobody listens, but she sings all the same
then I see her look at me

no title

look at him as he waits there for you
all dressed in black with nothing to share
except for what you need him to be

and don't worry yourself about what you'll do tomorrow
because tomorrow has nothing to do with today
except for what you need it to be

just look at me waiting, looking at you
all dressed in black with too much to share
except what I need you to be

still about a girl

held

she arrests me
her blonde hair sweeping across her back as she walks
when she moves by me
I can't help but look her way
she ties me up
my heart prisoner to this gorgeous girl

deep rays of sunshine is the color of her skin
she means Springtime to me
and quiet picnics under an apple tree
lost in a field of changing eyes and perfect smiles
calm mornings of coffee and muffins
no pressure for the day ahead

she's serenity
woolen blankets and cotton pillows
when I look at her, I see butterflies
orange wings flittering and white flowers willing to take her in
she's become a princess to me
she has but to ask and I will obey

just tell me
tell me what it is you want
what it is you need
I can make your wishes come true

just once in awhile

a friend told me he saw you last night
I'm glad he let me know
the memory of you danced over and all around me
the waves of recollection of the way you look when you're happy
the way your eyes turn to water with not a care in the world

I think of you all the time
and now, all the more
I miss you, Sandy
I do

though darkness may bathe me again in gray
I'll cling to the hope that maybe, just once in awhile
I'll be felt in your heart
maybe, just once in awhile
you'll remember my hands caressing your waist
if just once in awhile

to wait for you
hoping
wishing that your love will change and float over towards me
crying
wanting to know if I'm a part of the scrapbook of your life
maybe, just once in awhile, you'll turn to the page that is mine
maybe, just once in awhile, you'll miss me, too
if just once in awhile

I miss you, Sandy
I love you
maybe, just once in awhile, you'll love me, too

still about a girl

even then

three years ago…you and I shared our lives
and all that we needed to be
three years gone by
and I'm still thinking of you
about your love, your hope, and you
I love you, Ashley
still, after all this time
to spend another special day with you
would melt me
warm me
and bring true the connection between us
once in awhile, it's nice to know you think of me
'cause you were the girl, sweetie
and I'll love you until death comes between us
and even then
I'll love you all the much more

lest you forget

and when she sees me
she doesn't remember
and only sees the others that are around
it's turbulent, you see
the way this all feels
as if it didn't happen
just up and down

getting past you
that's what this is all about
and every time I see you
you bring me down

still about a girl

it is still there

at night when I close my eyes, I can see you
coming to me on flowered dreams
and each smile you give fills me with feathered warmth
making me shudder beneath my cool sheets

I see you drinking coffee with your friends
and how you are even more beautiful than before
that's when my heart sinks and I want to cry
'cause in the end, I'll never know why
how all I feel for you can be wrong

sometimes I think you weren't ready
and it felt like you fell in between
other times I think I fell too quickly
and you were overwhelmed by me

but deep inside you, I know you care
I just wish those feelings would come to light
just like they had before
when we were together, when I kissed you goodnight

I would give anything to be with you again
even wait a thousand years
I just can't help but break and cry
when I try to be your friend

please don't say that I can't see you anymore
please don't tell me to stop loving
every part of you
every piece that is you
and the things you want to be
I just need you to be patient with me

it's fair to say you feel what you feel

and it's fair to say that I feel what I feel
but if it was my love that drove you away
isn't that okay? 'cause I could watch what I say

and no matter what is now
I know...
I know
it is still there between you and me

still about a girl

miss you

where are you?
truly
I miss you
left here with these phantom designs
swirling whispers, hearing you say you love me
need this
need you
it's been nearly five years but Time has lost meaning
I can still smell your breath from when you leaned in to kiss me
peppermint
cherry
iced-tea
your lips were so soft
tender
you sent shockwaves through me
sometimes I can't remember us
and it hurts me
breaks frail feelings into shattered memories
to want you
to want this
crumbling to dust
tears in my eyes
darling dear, girl of mine
was mine
where are you
truly
miss you
decorate me in blue
in numbers you call your own
walk with me
don't run
live
surface in me again tonight
I miss you so

your words of color make me think of you

alone in my world of book and pen
your memory washes over me again
as the ink drips onto the page
I can feel our dance, there, upon the stage
for inside myself I can hold you
and keep you warm, safe, like you do
my heart

each morning I awake, hoping I'll receive some sign you're all right
each afternoon, I think of you, wondering if you might
call me that evening, just so I could hear your voice
and make a choice
to let our today fade into yesterday
or to let our friendship take us away
together

in the quiet hours of the night, I read
those tender verses telling of your needs
I want to know your heart, what you feel inside
do you care for me or do you want to be let be, only to hide?
your gentle voice and words of color
make mine seem for another
but what if, when your heart is calm
if we grew together, love pulling us along
into eternity

Tracy, there's so much I want to give
so much to make a life where I live
knowing you with adoration sincere
to assure you that there's no more fear
not even in tomorrow
for whatever Fate has in store for us both
Mother Nature has already sworn an oath:
we have only today

still about a girl

our tomorrow may never come
and our yesterday will never fade away

things change

the sun had only risen yesterday
but fell asleep today

still about a girl

she needs to be free...but He is here

I can see it there behind her eyes
through their gorgeous hazel disguise
shining as if solar flared
hinting of something with need to declare

see, you're a caterpillar, hiding in a cocoon
wondering which day for us is still oh so soon
to release your love out of its shell
and relish in the joy you had known so well

free yourself, sweetie, free yourself, dear
heart first, mind next, heart first, trust next
free yourself, sweetie, free yourself, dear
love first, love next, you first, me next

is it your fear that makes you want to leave?
one month or two, to find Who you believe?
here is something you should know
He is with you, no matter where you go

He is here, now as you read
He is with you, whenever you need
a Friend, a Love, a Place to stay
I know He is here, so please, don't go away

free yourself, darling, free yourself, my love
to work together, to build something strong
free yourself, darling, free yourself, my love
because it is you I've needed so long

and I won't know what to do...

...when you're gone

you held me, we sang

we sang together, me and you
words written by another, yet all ringing true

we held each other
dancing to a British tune
with your warm cheeks pressed against mine
and for the sweetest of moments
I felt your heart

we sang, sang songs of love
with your voice touching me the most
whether your words were true or just read from a screen
it doesn't matter
because, in the end, I got to hear you sing
and had you hold me
and held me
you held me

still about a girl

it's okay

it's okay to grieve
it's okay to try
it's okay to love
even after they're gone

Mr. Fuchs's time unkempt

Bitterness glistens upon my brow,
dripping into my eyes, blinding me from you—
and all that I remember becomes lost in fragmented memory
and washed up dreams on a shore of disillusions and muddled truths.

It's been so along since we've been together
that I can't remember what had been real
and what had been you.
And what hadn't been me but the one I make myself out to be.

Like chains forbidding a ship to explore,
so does the past cling to me.
So does history become a hopeful future,
as I wait for those glorious days to arrive again.

You've sailed on, though,
and I've been left behind,
standing on the rocks that gouge my feet
with the notions of you coming back again.

But to press on against this tasteless, pungent world,
crying like the babe you will share with another—
it tears me to pieces
of mirrored reflections of a better day.

I've loved you all these years, my lady,
but it's been the you from time unkempt.
And I've been in love with myself,
but it's been the me you've never met.

The days and years roll on like thundering hooves
through the desert of my soul,
and my throat is parched, cracked, thirsty
for the love that passed—pressed—on time and again.

still about a girl

O dreary thought! Abandon me now!
Or let a dreary death claim me
for I can't live this way anymore,
hiding in a childish wishing world
where the sky is always blue, the grass green,
and where your eyes always shine upon me.

her fire within

it's the way she carries herself
chin up
pressing the world beneath her
her eyes wander, looking elsewhere
perhaps to him, and what he took away
she seems warm, but only at her center
beneath a blanket of stone
and cool winds
she hides, buries herself within that place she keeps secret
only one, perhaps two, have ventured there before
when she smiles she looks like she wants to cry
as if rising cheeks hurt her
remind her
of what things were like
in her ears she hears the echo of his voice
his words calming her, reassuring her
and for a moment, if you look closely
you can see the cozy fire within
and you want to go home

stream (16)

Things are supposed to be getting on now. But they aren't. I'm still hung up on you. We haven't been together for four years; that's one higher than the number of months we were together. Everyday is about you.

I'm with someone now. And she's great. But sometimes, when I rest my head on her lap and close my eyes, I imagine it's you stroking my hair or running your fingers across my cheek. Then I'm happy. It's not fair to her, I know, but I can't help but keep you alive inside of me.

It's pretty much safe to say that my life is ruined, always lost in that place of the past. Or maybe I've brainwashed myself into thinking that I'll always love you. Yet...there was that one time where I saw you at my coffee shop a year and a half ago. We talked and it was like we never left that place that was ours. It was like nothing had ever come between us and we were back into it again.

But that was then and this is now, some would say. I agree, as I'm trying to look forward to the future.

But you're always there. Will you ever go? A part of me wants you to, but an even bigger part of me doesn't.

And the problem is that you hate me. You think I'm a creep, the classic obsessive ex-boyfriend. But I'm not. I was just honest with you when I said that being without you makes me want to die. That's all. But, I suppose, hearing such a thing would scare anybody. It scares me, too.

Will it get better, and can I ever say that I love you enough to let you go? Maybe one day, as I'm caring for you more and more as each day passes. Maybe I'll reach that point where I couldn't possible love you more.

Maybe then I'll be able to say good-bye.

long time

the hours seem to tick away
as I dream of a better place
of you amongst flowers
these pain shaping hours
but I can't sleep no more
behind this heart wrecked door
waiting for you to come along

I got nothin' and you ain't got no reason
to fly over my skies
to fly over my skies

I wrap myself in a quilt of you
hey, man, look, I got nothin' to do
as time goes
only she knows
where I've gone
where I've been
but I can't sleep at night
knowing you've lost the bright light
when are you coming home?

I got nothin' and you ain't got no reason
to fly over my skies
to fly over my skies

I got nothin' and you ain't got no reason
to fly over my skies
to fly over my skies

(I am so lonely
and you're gone)

still about a girl

not done

and as summer fills me up again
I remember the first time you said hello
and the way the shadows melted
when you came walking up to me

you took my hand and brought it to your face
my skin brushing against potter's gold
and your warmth took me in
wrapping me in wonder, in light—oh

you filled me up today
with color and dream's candlelight
in daisy cream and piano song
come to me once again

you kissed my hand
with cracked lips so thin
and said to me, your eyes bathed in green mint
come on, baby, let me in, so I can be all over you

and when this girl falls into pretty colors
she reminds me of another
and all those quiet things that only she seems to see
"It's the rhythm," she says, "but in you more than me."

happy anniversary

I usually remember these things
but I forgot about you
and I'm thankful, too
that I had

so much time is spent in misery
relieving the old days
relieving those old ways
with you

because you took all that I had
everything there was for me to give
everything for you so that you might live
with something a little better than what you knew before

but it all counted for naught
and, well, I don't mind
because I got a better kind
of someone that came after you

so happy anniversary, sweetie
I hope you're happy that it's undone
because a year's already come and gone
and I can't remember you anymore

still about a girl

simply stated

Hesitantly, she said, "I promise to love you
"from now until the end of eternity."
And I believed her, believe me,
because I loved her, too.
So much for trust.

never know

every time she smiles, I wonder if she can hear it
hear the tum-tum-tumbling rice of a canasta
every time she moves
how could I express the laughter I feel when I see her?
and how, for a brief moment, everything seems to be okay?
I can't and she'll never know
never know
never know the words I wish to speak

sometimes, when I play guitar, I can see her dance
her music, the shake-shake-shaking of canastas
the rhythm of her eyes, her thoughtful glance
and a secret moment where she speaks to me without sound
only to remind me of sunset
can I hold her? if only once?
no, for she is already held
I wish I was held
but I am alone
shake-shake-shake
she makes me shake
she will always make me shake

stream (9)

I keep thinking about you. Keep thinking with a quick heart. It beats my thoughts. Over and over, again and again.

You work seven floors below me, seven floors away. It's such a distance, but I love the fact that you're near. I love how I think of you. Over and over, again and again.

I think about your eyes and the little glow of affection they emit. And especially your smile. I know I probably sound cliché but those are the features that make you beautiful.

It breaks my heart to know that you belong to someone else. If only I could take his place if just for a day. I wonder what he has that I don't. Maybe it's my beard? Maybe you think it's too long?

You're back again, in my mind's eye. Your image; over and over, again and again. I can hear your voice inside my head. An echo of what is seven floors below. A voice which warms my ears.

I guess my question is, do you think of me?

day to night

if I could take the sunshine out of your life
I would
and replace it with moonlight
to accent our mood

if I could change the way clouds puff the sky
I'd try
and replace them with stars
so that you would cry

you'd cry for me, cry for you, then cry for me again
I'd hold you then
and kiss your cheeks while I stroked your chin

if I could take away the nightmares of day
I might
replace them with dreams of white roses
and you at night

and at last, if I left the orange of twilight
I'd take you
away from here to my world at night
you and I, two
then one

you would cry as you go, tears streaking down your cheeks
but don't cry kitten, no more, don't weep
for we are together, here, with our dreams
now, when the day had turned to night

still about a girl

saturday

it was a Saturday in October
when the leaves ceased to fall
it was a Tuesday in January
an evening I lost it all

since then there are no more days
and I am out of time
I wish that I could feel the sun
and all that used to be mine

an echo is all you are
and everything to me
your glorious red of kool-aid
and the whisper of our sea

I have a cot in the back of my mind
where our memories lay to rest
and dream of life in all its splendor
and all its nightmares, I guess

sheltered by the black stars above
and lonely beneath this monster in me
dead to our clouds of Superman blue
and you, my serendipity

will you remember what it was like to fly?
or how there was air beneath your toes?
or the way that we had touched each other
my lips upon your nose?

another Saturday in October
another day beneath the sun
everyday that has passed has said

that you
Ashley
were the one

still about a girl

when she sleeps

it is when she dreams that I love her the most
for that is when she is safest from me
and all the things I can't forget

and it is when she opens her eyes
that I become lost in her
to do all the things I'll regret

she takes me in, all the time
and I can't seem to take myself away
from when I need her to stay

it's those things that she says that keeps me awake
and the words that she means
when she has nothing to say

the way she laughs is what gets to me
each time her eyes smile in that fading way
that makes me feel human inside

and I can't help but wonder
wonder, wish, and know
how it is she's got nothing to hide

she's just her, always
she just the "way it is"
and I shudder

and I'm just me, always
I'm just the "way it shouldn't be"
and she shudders
because she knows that this weathered soul
is no more than a needy child
begging for her never to run along

A.P. Fuchs

I wish I was her
more than me
never to fear anything to go wrong

if I was her
it would be easy
and it would be "OK"

and if she was me
it would be harder
but it would be "just another day"

she would get it
and I would leave
and she would look prettier that way

still about a girl

coffee, cigarettes, 2AM

alone in our coffee shop
waiting for you
it seems like you're taking forever to get here
I've had five cups of coffee
three cigarettes
and the clock keeps crawling, never reaching 2AM
I can't believe how much I miss you
why do you have to be so perfect?
why can't you be like the other girls
the ones who always end up leaving me behind?

see, there's this thing between you and me
and...it's not love because love is far too simple a word to describe it
but whatever it is, it's making me crazy
making me change my life so I can be a better man for you
perhaps more deserving
perhaps more of what you need

you found me when I had nothing left to give
you found me when I was ready to leave this life
you can't fly or bend steel bars with your bare hands
you don't even wear a red skirt, a blue shirt,
or a red towel draped over your shoulders
yet, you saved me
helping me to see that I can live in this sad Metropolis
and live with my wasted life

I don't expect miracles from you or a commitment for us
to always be together
the moments we have are the moments I hold dear
when you're not around
it's the memories that help me breathe, help me make do
with what I have

my watch says you're going to be here in five minutes
2AM is coming
and even if you're late, I still have three cups of coffee and ten more cigarettes left
but, more specifically, a lonely heart
waiting to be filled

still about a girl

and if there's time

no easy way to forsake this shame
no easy way to find our names
in golden sand
on the land
away from all those waves

and if there's time
she will come down from the waves
and wash over me always
and every time
I see her
she will begin to fall into me

come down from your seabird
come on down from all you've heard
about those things kept secret
have you remembered me yet?
have you seen the white on your skin?

don't forget this, little one
don't let go of running in the sun
just let my feathers take you in
just let yourself
let yourself
just let yourself win

and if there's time
she will fall down from her waves
and wash over me always
and every time
I see her
she will slip slowly into me

and as the years go by

don't say I didn't try
to let you know
how love works slow
and how you still remember me

don't forget this, my darling
don't let go of your swing
just let my wings take you in
just let yourself
let yourself
just let yourself begin

and if there's time
she will fly down from her waves
and wash over me always
and every time
I see her
she will drift gently into me

to find out how to say I'm sorry, dear
to see how things have changed here
to find out what you're missing now
to see what was yours and how
you missed your chance

for one last walk under the starlight
for one last kiss goodnight
for one last hand held in mine
for one last love for all time

only if there's time

still about a girl

can't find a way

got to find a way, away from this poet's life
got to find me a little sanctity
need to walk away from my desert sky
got to walk away from me

sitting beneath the warmth of candles
beside the crumpled pages of my dreams
I think about you tonight
and why I gave all of me

shivering with the dangers of love, the way it seemed complete
shuddering with the blanket of melted you
I can't see a way
a way out of here
there's no way out of here

want to find me a little piece of belonging
want to find a railroad back home
need to see my feet beneath the dirt
want to find the better part of being alone

standing still on the pavement of my yard
beside the fallen leaves of the breeze
I think about you miles before
I fall down upon my knees

quivering with time and waves of pain
shaking with the hot towels of better days
I can't find a way
a way out of here
'cause you're the way back home

upon the ceilings of pastel blue
I see you clear, sparkling and true

and I know
I know
there's no way back to you

still about a girl

a love poem

you are more than I could have ever wanted
more than I could have ever needed
to sit beside you
walk beside you
to spend time with you
I can't even acknowledge their own special magnificence
I wonder who dreamed of you and made you real
I wonder who had crafted you, a flower so immaculate
ever so beautiful
I'm so in love with you
I love you so, so much
and I can't even speak when we're together
can't find the words to express all that I feel
I pray for the day you'll take me in your arms
and finally, finally, I can tell you that I want to say
need to say, so badly want to say
Sandy, you're indescribable
your tender skin makes my hands cry out to touch
your soft lips…I want to kiss…forever and all the time
to hold you, feeling every single breath you take
feel your body shudder as your heart races
to smell your hair, your neck, your hands
and revel in the pleasure that they store
I can't see into tomorrow and another day without you
or through the tears which wet my eyes when I'm awake
there is no yesterday or the pain of someone who had tried to be you
trying to capture me like you do
I beg you, down on one knee, to take me into your heart
I beg you to cradle me, kiss my cheek,
and run you fingers down my back
there is nothing without you
there is anything with you
everything
to know that you care for me steals all that I am

to be touched how you've touched me
to be changed how you've changed me
you are my miracle
I'd rather go my whole life and not see another
for you are what love is
love was
and everything love will be
though I already love you, I fall further each day
falling so much more in love with you
to see you smile in my mind's eye makes me smile
and hearing your voice in my ears fills my heart
I'd give anything, do anything, be anything, if it meant
that I could be yours
for what is being alive without you?
it is just existing, not living, each moment pained
with all I can never have
you protect me when I'm afraid
and heal me when I'm sick
you are all the precious purities of all God's women
the greatest girl for somebody to know and love
I can't stand this loneliness any longer
just merely sitting on the sidelines, knowing that to play with you
is all I want, need, and love
you are so wonderful
you are all that is pretty and nice and good
tell me that I can tell you more
and the way you warm me when you're near
to be one with you, the very thought makes me shake
because you overwhelm me
what can I say?

still about a girl

never what she needed me to be

when she sang she smiled
you could see it
joy abundant
on stage was where she was meant to be

bringing her to that singing room
that place
I am glad to have partaken
in handing her the comfort she needs

so many times I held her hand
so many more we sang to each other
where have you gone; where haven't you gone
let me take you there

three years have gone by yet
still tearful eyes break me inside
I'm sorry I couldn't be what you were looking for
I'm even sorrier for being me

self-pity absent
pity for you brilliant
never was who you needed me to be
you were everything I needed to see

and have
and hold
and love…
and love

echo's shoulder

waiting for Ashley to come 'round
her starlight never fades away
just gives itself in reams of truth
filling this darkness where I stay

girl you
boy me
laugh out loud
there is only she

on waking mornings when blue arises
beauty and fallen leaves; she is amazing
on tea-filled afternoons
I'm always stargazing

blackness is loneliness
the color of her forgotten voice
brokenness and shatters
seems my only choice

angels fly, they say, with soft cotton wings
filling the skies and lives and days
sweetening everything
in dreams of al[l]ways

on echo's shoulder I'll sit and wait
wait for that ferry's sound
I only pray it's not too late
the day Ashley comes 'round

stream (5)

I wish I could see you right now. Instead I'm looking upon the reflection of myself in a cup of coffee.

I take a deep drag from my cigarette, the coarse taste of it reminding me that I shall never drink from your lips again. I'll never be able to taste that special tenderness that only you can emit.

It's times like this I wonder if you ever wish to see me. Do you gaze into your cup of hot chocolate longing to see my face? Or do you long to see his, my replacement, whoever that might be. Have you shelved my picture in a forgotten drawer of your mind? Or am I destined to reside with your unfinished thoughts and memories of a pain forgotten?

Fallon, my dreams echo of your love. Each moment of my life is soaked with your image. I long to see you again, if only for a moment. After all, I suppose that's what we were. A moment. A tender ripple in the pool of time. I have to ask, will you ever cause the water to stir again or have you dropped your pebble on the shore and walked away?

'til you came along my way

I can't remember when
my solace began to change
and life filled with a white cotton life
with colored leaves and rainbows again

all I knew
was years without you
and your moments without me

November cracked our clouds of gray
and calmed our rivers of storm and time
I can't believe I heard you say
that now my hands are untied

all my life I had it all
and all that is said to sustain
but there was crying
there was dying
'til you came along my way
setting love the way it should be
when we found yourself in me

I'm clinging to the faith in your eyes
and the satin that is in your cheeks
I hope and pray
hope and love
hope and hope that it is me you seek

there is no bottom, 'cause I'm drowning inside of you
you are true
there is no flight, because I'm falling, falling, falling for you
and you
and you
I keep falling for you

still about a girl

no matter where your voice leads
I'll be there beside you
collapsed to my knees
giving you all that I am...and will be
again

all my life I didn't have it all
or anything said to sustain
but there was trying
there was crying
then you turned my night into day
setting love the way it should be
no, "you," nor, "I"...only, "we"
just you and me
with Him and love

and together
side by side
I know
we will be
we will be
just you and me

my princess

across the folds of sand, my princess walks
brown eyes beneath the sun
skin glistening with sweat
she leaves tender footprints in her wake
and wears a veil to protect herself from the desert winds
silk fabric against silk skin

over the dune is where her mystery lies
something warm, not yet seen
yet she knows what it is

with her fingers, she brushes the brown curls from her brow
tiny beads of morning dew beneath
"Over the dune," she says,
"that's where he'll be."

her legs shudder
acknowledging the distance she must cross
and how the hot sand will burn her feet
she must reach him,
reach him and drink the water of his lips
but it is too far
too hot
and the wind blows stronger

she falls to her knees and removes her veil
her chapped lips kiss the sand
she whispers his name into the hot floor
hoping that he will hear
he does, ever so quietly

by then, my princess lies asleep
waiting for tomorrow
waiting for him to come

still about a girl

then...is better now

you look at me the same way you always do
eyes awash with silver, red highlights of uncertainty
when I return your gaze I wonder who it is you're waiting for
who you need and what you'll allow yourself to have
so many forks in the road, isn't there?
nice or mean
good or bad
tender or degrading
all appealing yet revolting all the same
do you miss him, the man you dreamed of so long ago?
do you see him, day to day, hiding within the people you meet?
there is a place I remember you
the same place I forget about me
that special place, buffered by time
long days change us
hard days break us
but in the end
some things remain the same
and it just gets better

the day we were supposed to meet

it was sometime in September
the first day that I met her
out at the coffee shop down the street
she looked at me, almost crying
she spoke to me, nearly dying
the day we were supposed to meet

and if I can't stay here
with you in my arms
please know that I'll go
and be alone once again

Sandy tells me of a ring of gold
and all the empty promises she was told
while she drags on a cigarette
her eyes tell me of her sorrow
and how she doesn't wanna live 'til tomorrow
to see what else she'll forget

and if I can't kiss her
and touch her cheeks again
please know that I'll go
to be alone
just like before

her hair smells red like flowers
perfumed with roses and fresh spring rain showers
there, inside of me
Sandy, please tell me that I'll be okay
that somehow my life will sink back to yesterday
and all that we should be

you said that you're shaking
and inside you're breaking

still about a girl

and my love is frightening and soothing all the same
that you won't have me
but you need me
lost in indecision

and if I can't hold you
and go down on one knee
please know that I'll go
'cause I'm always alone
you're making me feel alone
I have no home
you are my home

please, will you cry for me

Sandy smiles

Sandy tells me she gets too much sleep
and how she can't find the strength to wake
because she dreams of roses, lilies, all that is sweet
and of blue rain and snow

with Eden dancing behind her eyes
and the kisses of wine to her lips
she rescues me when the shadow tries
to steal me from all of this

clashing against an occulent sky, bleeding her number four
Sandy smiles, laughs and says: "if only you could love me more"
and hidden somewhere in a secret quilt
I whisper what she yearns to hear
my arms, hands, love and heart, drawing her ever so near
to the piece of her inside of me and all that should be...
only to towel her eyes

she is crying
she is laughing
she is loving
she is changing
my Sandy, a beautiful story with a happy ending
forever and ever
and ever no more
only for you
only for me
only for you
only for...

still about a girl

giving in

I feel like I'm sinking to a whole other level
the one where it becomes all about me
and I will refuse
because I don't want to use
whatever is left of me
to make me feel better
as I try to forget her
and fall asleep
never to dream

a past origin

it's the stinging tongue of separation
that reminds me of this desperation
of reaching out to find you again

a space between us
bringing us ever the closer more
and ever the more the same

when you look at me I can see it
the gentle chime
of your thoughts as they rhyme
rhyme along with mine

and how you found voice to say what you mean
and sing of your most glorious dreams

so many fond memories of the immaculate touch
so many nightmares where I didn't mean as much
as one of us thought

sure, this thing called time could be counted
instead, I'm content to say
we've only just started

still about a girl

is it me?

melancholy draws upon her lips
as if she is bathing in the habitual water of discomfort
is it me? maybe. after all, I'm not that great a catch
is it her? maybe. after all, she knows I'm not that great a catch

on some days we are linked
on others, I feel like I'm the only bond
is it me? maybe.
is it her? maybe, too.
see, the thing is...I love her
more than more could ever be
more than more should ever be
is it me? yes.
is it her? it's always been her.

and, I suppose
her
it will always be

you are yesterday

it's time to say
say stay away
away from me today
you are yesterday

you're gone
gone, gone away
gone
gone away today

you, you whisper quietly
and I speak so gently
and you look so lovely
you are yesterday

come, come to me and say
that you loved that day
that you loved that day

you're gone
gone, gone away
gone
gone away today

things change so suddenly
I'm no longer me
oh, can't you see
I am yesterday

I am yesterday
you are yesterday
I am yesterday

still about a girl

Fallon's song

I haven't been here
for a long, long time
it's about time
I rise for you

slow time passes
and I see you
always there for me

always there for me

and I'm falling down for you
falling down for you
face down for you
all for you

despite the things I've done
despite this song I sing
every bell is rang for you
every prayer is meant for you

and as your presence floats on by
I can't help but fall and cry
but I sing this song for you
for you

'cause you were always there for me

and I'm falling down for you
falling down for you
face down for you
all for you

and I'm falling down for you

falling down for you
face down for you
all for you

falling away

your sand has drifted to the bottom of the glass
small peppered granules of the past
the vestibule shutters beneath our touch
three months of love isn't much
but it had made a difference
in my life

with careful thoughts you wonder
if the hourglass could be flipped over, ponder
for if you reset the hands of time
I will be yours and you will be mine
but you won't take that chance
or even give me a second glance
so instead, like the sand
I will fall away
day by day
fall away

something I had to say

she comes up to me and asks how I've been
as if she could tell that I haven't slept for four days
I tell her I'm fine and compliment her
for today she looks beautiful—like everyday before

when I look at her, I grow still
each moment lasting just long enough for me to take her in
take in her eyes that grow soft around their edges
the subtle curves at the corners of her lips
at the rays of sunset which flow through her hair

my thoughts and feelings thicken when I see her
as if she slows my every move and every beat of my heart
I remember the warm breeze that washed over me
the first time I saw her
the heated breeze that I still feel every time she looks my way

I feel like nothing before her
all that I am rinses away when she is near
maybe that's why I'm writing these things down instead of telling her
but I am not all words
only actions and displays
waiting for her hand to run across mine

if she knew, I wonder, if she knew...
what would she say to me? how would I touch her, if at all?
I want to hear her voice, her soothing sound
so the silence will stop humming in my ears

still about a girl

she keeps me warm

I was touched by wonder tonight
my heart dipping into her pool of life
for she knows what I see
the world as it shouldn't be
her love is formed like mine

she is frail, worn by the years of harm
her fingers delicate, like rose petals
and her skin, that of a porcelain doll
shining in the stars

her words move me
as I see myself in all that she has to say
my stomach aching from her truth
caught in a whirlwind of sudden adoration

she misses him, seeing him only in dreams
pleasant thoughts
fragile feelings
but don't worry, child
he misses you, too
he needs to hold you
to kiss you
to love you

though I may be the farthest thing from her mind
she is so close to me
here
where she has permeated me the most
in my heart, keeping me warm

and more

there's just all this crying over you
my brown-eyed friend
there's just all this trying to get you
to come back to me once again
I'm so sorry to you
I just don't know what I've done
I just wish I had somebody
to take me to the sun
and as these hours pass into days
I still remember the last time I saw you
and as these days turn into years
I was wondering if you remember me, too

'cause there's just no forgetting
all that you meant
to me
and there's all this regretting
from the time spent
with you

but I wouldn't have had it any other way
because you were worth
all that this life is made of
and more

still about a girl

angels are on earth

she folds me in
enveloping me with blonde hair, hazel eyes
her touch runs shivers through me
coating me with warm apprehension
angels are on earth

when she walks by
she wears a cloak made of rose petals
a refreshing scent lingering in her path
enrapturing me
angels walk among us

like cotton clouds
she rains upon me, bathes me in light, darkness
the colors in between swirling around me like a tornado
taking me away
she's an angel in every way

she smiles like a kitten, with tender eyes like a puppy
she brings new meaning to the word "perfection"
making all those that have come before her pale against her
rinsing them away in Heaven's light
my angel is on earth

don't fly away
don't ride along the clouds of home
stay with me, down here
in my life, in my heart
be my angel on earth

so carefully there

she looked like you
all baggy clothes and gorgeous hair
she smiled like you
a hint of secret in smooth cheeks

seeing her, I saw you
she, reaching into distant memory
drawing you out and placing you before me
sweet ecstasy

on the onset of realization
your revelation became clear
it's you, my love
you I need near

how can life be put on pause
and hope become my dream
when chances are there is no chance
of you again with me

she was you, I swear
and I just fell apart
I was me, unfortunately
that girl—she stole my heart

and gave it to you
to hold and care for
so carefully there
you, my angel
you

still about a girl

don't remind me

don't remind me that I miss you
every time light casts upon my face
and don't say, "believe me,"
and that, "it's better this way."

'cause it never changes
all that I feel
it never changes

so please tell me that you know the truth
of how much of me is somewhere in you

and if you deny me as
I turn gray and fall
just don't remind me
that I meant nothing at all

drawn in, thrown out

across the tales of beautiful night
she sits away from me, not looking back
sheltered from estranged times
I sink inside myself, pulled low and biting back tears
I don't want her to see me like this
but she will
she has
and it hasn't made a difference

often I speak of yesterday and the comfort it brings
but it is only that—yesterday, never to happen again
a tattered picture is all I am
ugly and easily cast away
I want her to repaint me
bring me back to elated dreams, mood-less eves

the will to speak is gone
drawn in, lost somewhere in the grief
and pain...and me
I want her to see me
to hear me, be near me
I'm shaking
I've been awake too long
always tired, always waiting...

...for this dream to come true

still about a girl

there is no fate

I don't believe our paths were meant to cross
I don't believe we were meant to fall in love then fall away
because there is no such thing as fate

I don't believe we are not meant to be together
and I don't believe that we are
because there is no such thing as fate

we found each other by chance
we were taken from each other by chance, too
because there is no such thing as fate

this business of "meant to bes" and "let fate decides"
is only a mere comforter
a mask
a blanket to make us feel better when we lose control
and lose those we love

it is a false hope
placed on something that doesn't exist
so that we can be reassured
that things will work out for the best

to trust in such superstition
deprives the human heart and mind
of what really matters
of what is really needed

I'm sick of people telling me it wasn't meant to be
or if we are meant to be together then we will
we all have choices
and all choices have consequences
all consequences spawn choices
because there is no such thing as fate

we have a choice, you and I
the question is: what are going to do
when we have no place left to go
and only each other to turn to
we have a choice, you and I
so let's just wait and see
if you and I are meant to be

stream (3)

It's odd now, seeing you again. Which each thoughtful glance I give, I'm reminded of the hurt I caused you. The way you so willingly gave yourself to me and I to you even though my heart belonged to another.

You casually display your stomach across the way and I see how you've got your belly button pierced, an idea which you told me once. My heart falls as I see your smooth skin again, the perfectly tanned midsection that I've grown to love. It's too bad my words can never form as before and my feelings never float over to you again.

I feel shamed, alone and naked in your presence when I see how you've moved on. The truth is, I haven't. Your visage still haunts my memory. I catch myself wondering if we had met under a different light in a different time, if any of this would have come to pass.

I can now only look at you from a distance even though my heart feels close. How do you see me now? Does that magnetic pull still linger inside your chest?

If secretly you do care for me, shall I never know? Will you protect yourself from me and pray I never strike again? I suppose we all have shields. You, your vagueness of words and I, hair and smoke. Maybe one day we'll let our masks slip and allow ourselves to meet again.

Until then, I will remain aside and think of you as a lost friend.

over

you felt bad
when I told you of the sadness you wrought
I felt bad
when you told me of the feelings I stirred
it seems as though things hadn't been
yet occurred all the same
after all, my heart bleeds
and sings of you, me, all we were
I miss you
that hasn't changed
and neither will you
...and neither will you
...

still about a girl

her cheek rests in my hand

She says to me, "What do you see, see in me?
"Why would you waste your tongue only to share?"
Carefully, I take her cheek in my hand,
her smooth skin resting against mine,
and I reply, "Instead of hiding beneath the shadows of time past,
"I'd rather bring forth my light to you, now, just so that you knew
"that you are loved,
"cared for,
"deeply."

She smiles at this, a small grin,
eyes suddenly washed over in quiet tears.
"I will never understand," she says, "never know why
"you want me in your arms."
I place her other cheek in my other hand, my eyes growing soft.
She's scared.
Scared of what I might say.
But that's okay. I'll hold her until she stops quivering.

Pursing my lips, I offer her my heart, and say, "You don't have to
"understand, my love. There is no need.
"What matters is I love you. That's all."

She closes her eyes in understanding, a single tear sliding to my hand.
With my thumb, I wipe it away, lean forward, and kiss her brow.
She opens her eyes, something having changed.
Within the instant of an eternity of a heart's leap, I know what it is.
Once again, she smiles, putting the circle of time on hold.
That's when I'm told,
"I understand."

way back when (one more time)

you realize how much you miss someone
when you dream of them
and you see what you should have done
way back when
and how you let her slip away
without meaning to

if only I could be with her again

still about a girl

play, night, love

there was our time down by the lake
I remember thinking, "This is how it's gonna stay."
it was night and we were alive
I held you then in monotonous sighs
we played on the swing-set, the jungle-gym, too
my mind thinking, thinking
thinking only of you
so bad, it seems, to go back to then
that time apart from this life, the special times when
all we knew was freedom from ourselves
open books, no broken shelves
security in love, security in you
O, Ashley, why do I dream
dream
dream, sleep and dream
keep dreaming of you?

can't forget

it's late at night
and I'm remembering the feelings again
and this swollen emptiness inside
just keeps multiplying
growing
as I grow older
you get to a point where you're sick of it all
and you wish you could just move on
but what are we with our past?
because, without yesterday,
there wouldn't be a today
I'm sick of being sick
swathed in self-pity and
plagued with a mind that can't forget
and I hate myself for thinking of you
especially since I have someone else
yet
if it were offered to change the past
so that you and I never met
I wouldn't take it
I couldn't
because forgetting you would be forgetting myself
and I wouldn't be me anymore
but at least I'd stop hating myself
maybe the self-pity would be gone
maybe not
because someone even more beautiful than you
might have come along
and ruined me
more than you ruined me
again, I'm just sick of being sick
swarmed with self-pity
and woe-is-mes
I just wish I could forget you

still about a girl

and move on
and live
just like everyone else
in a life that is not yesterday
but only today
without you
but then
I'd be without me
and who I am
the man you left behind

if you were near (I'm at a loss)

it's coming on again
I feel it at the back of my head
the dreams
of this girl from long ago

but I didn't know
that loving could be this hard
and the letting go all the more harder
than it already is

because I miss that kiss
from nearly four years ago
that touch of beauty
that keeps me company to this day

I just wish there was a way
to go on further
and leave her behind
instead of always feeling her near

it's just that she's so dear
to me, that she'll always be a part of me
whether I like it or not
whether she likes it or not

but I just forgot
how to love in the now
because I'm still loving back then
it's all for this girl who's gone away

yet if she came to me today
instead of at night like she's known to do
I think I would crumble
because her presence is that thick

still about a girl

I'm thick
dense where it matters most
in that place beneath the sweater
where red and hurt pump through

just wish I knew
how to leave it be
and let it go
without always waiting for her to come back to bed

stream (17)

You can dream of a thousand ways to die. A thousand means of torture. But there is only one torment. One filled with need, with the desire to change it, to right a wrong from so long ago. The torment is a haunting memory, one that lingers and cannot be shaken away. It plagues your mind like an itch doomed to be ever-present, as you cannot reach it to scratch. If only the clock's hands would reverse themselves, spin backward to that time where you had the chance to right your wrong, to not drive her away, to tell her...you are sorry. History cannot be rewritten. Only the future can be determined. But she is not there, in your future. You are without her, for only to bring her there, you would have to return to the past, take her hand, and guide her forward.

still about a girl

the edge

I've walked this edge for a dozen years
each careful footfall a gentle step towards you
so many times I've thought of falling
thought of drifting downward into your chasm of night
so I could see you watch me, watch me as I fall, fall away

right now this canyon's edge spans forever
for I fear I will never meet you at the end
dust crumbles and sand crushes beneath my feet
some spilling over into your afterlife
speckles of my love for you

how long shall I teeter for I see my balance waning?
you've walked alongside me but never offered a helping hand
my hand is extended out to you now
will you take it
or shall I fall?

random (though sane)

wearing thin
sleep becoming my obsession
hungry for that little place that is mine
where I can always be with you

it's getting harder again
I thought I was strong
stronger than this
but, I suppose, I must wear on

one thing to dream
another to do
one thing to pretend
that it's okay, fine, all is in hand

but how much longer must I lie
bathing myself in the darkness of hope
and the light of "what if?"
and "if only"

just so tired these days
waiting for home to become real
home to become
just simply to become

gratitude is what I must remember
thankfulness that I'm here
though starving
tired and weary

keep pressing, pushing
more waiting
I am becoming
I am strong

still about a girl

I haven't forgotten me
unlike you
and I'll always remember
how you fell asleep next to me

I'll always remember

poem undone

she comes on in
and sits right down
across from me
and then she smiles at me
and I fall apart completely

she knows she's a long, long way from home
all the way over, all the way gone, but home still the same
but, little darling, don't be afraid
cuz over here I've got it made
over here the rain bathes you in sun beams and everglades

bringing you in
to where you want to be
and all you have to do
is ask me to hold you
bring you in, draw you near, in ways you're not used to

dream of lions and sleeping lambs
let me see you smile when you can
soft skin rises, cheeks so smooth and clean
I tell you, girl, you don't know what I mean
when I say you're the prettiest girl I've ever seen

age defies
goes away and separates
but in years gone by, when things change
your heart shudders, feelings rearrange
into a fuzzy quilt, warm, foreign and strange

still about a girl

you're not alone

back to where I started before
to writing alone and smoking away
I tell the tales and ideas of a better life
and how much I wish I existed on the page

tired from living without anything
drained and numb to any affection for life
I sit and stare in a blank room completely unaware
because I don't know any better than to live in my memories

every time I see you now I grieve and mourn
longing for the chance to read you one last poem
and tell you that I love you, kiss your forehead
and squeeze your hand
just so that you know that even though I am alone, you can never be

for I am always with you

up to this place

just to go to sleep, somewhere inside
just to go to sleep, not alone
just to go to sleep when I want someone
just to go to sleep in place of my own

she surrounds me just like angels do
she surrounds me like the colors of the rain
and if you asked me, quietly
I'd be with her once again

inside these walls of tattered time
in these days that go on by
I keep thinking about this angel of mine
and how she takes me high

up to this place
where the shadows never leave me
up to this place
where the quiet reminds me
that I am so lonely

just come on over, baby
just come on over to me
just come on over because you want someone
just come on over and let it be

she surrounds me like blankets do
she surrounds me like the colors of a dangerous sky
and if you said to me, tenderly
I'd fall down to her and ask her why

inside these thoughts of mine
in these waking moments of a dream
I keep thinking about this angel of mine

still about a girl

and how she's not what she seems

up to this place
where the shadows wrap their arms around me
up to this place
where the dancers remind me
that I'm known to be lonely

just let yourself feel
just let yourself decide
just let yourself be real
just let yourself die
just let yourself, baby
just let yourself, honey
just let yourself
fall into me

you walked away

I can't seem to focus
on what I came here to do
and between sips of coffee
all I can think of is you
and how you turned me away

from a corner, hidden in the dark
I sink into the pain of your shallow eyes
delving deeper
into your love in disguise
and how you threw me away

what could I have possibly done
to have you drift away from me
I used to be your everything
but only second best
to what you wanted me to be
just so you could walk away

I gave you so much
of myself
I gave you more
than he gave you before
yet, you'd rather say
that we won't have today
or any dream on its way

if love is pure and true and white
why did you leave me
alone, lost in the night
to be a prisoner of your voice
as if I had a choice
I just couldn't go away

still about a girl

I loved you the first time it rained
and when the hour turned to "our"
when you smelled of a bride's flower
and joy replaced our pain

in the end, I became no more than yesterday
while you turned to tomorrow
and I had to watch
and I had to feel you
when I couldn't breathe
the day you went away

Sandy, what if?

Sandy smiles
she is sitting next to me
I'm holding her close
just to kiss the top of her head
and ask...

what if you grew brighter than the sun and dazzled me once again?
what if, as the days go by, I fall even more in love with you?
what if our kisses were deposits of you into me and me into you?
what if we laughed together 'til our stomachs were sore,
then we laughed again?
what if your voice keeps ringing in my ears, helping me sleep?
what if you held me as if a baby, and I never let you go?
what if it started to rain and I had no place to go,
would you stay with me outside?
what if I could fly, where would you let me take you?
what if each moment was the first time we ever met,
forever making all we share so refreshingly new?
what if I couldn't get tired of you?
what if we played like children, and wrestled in the snow?
what if you fell for me, how would you know?
what if today is our tomorrow and our tomorrow our today?
what if I made you smile so you could light up the room?
what if I wanted to keep you, somewhere secret inside of me?
what if it was always you and me, and me and you?
what if you were crying and I cried for you?
what if I held you and you held me...forever?
what if we had nothing to do, would you be bored?
what would you say if I said that I loved you?

stream (8)

The radio is playing our song.

I hate it. Not the song but the fact that every time I hear it, I remember the phone call when we decided it would be ours.

Just when I think I'm over you, our song always has a way of bringing me back. It played on our first date and it was always playing on your stereo when I phoned you.

I suppose memories are a good thing but for me they become nightmares. Recollections of something I can never have.

When you hear our song, do you think of me? Do you remember the way we laughed together in your car as you drove us to that coffee shop so long ago?

Maybe not all the time but I'm sure sometimes you do. You cannot be that callous even though you formed a tough layer of skin between us.

It's over.

That what the radio said. Our song has changed to something else.

I don't want it to come on again.

all these things (just for you)

close your sleepy eyes
lay your head down
just fall away with me
into that quiet place
where the things you need
come to life
come to your heart
and take you away inside

imagine delicate hands
wrapped around you
delicate words
filling your ears
imagine someone who cares for you
and never lets you down

close off your heart to me
open up your eyes to
all that I have for you
just let yourself fall away with me
into your quiet place
where the things you need
come to life
come to your heart
and take you away inside

imagine tender things
all around you
tender things like teddy bears
giving you love
imagine someone who adores you
and never gives you up

all these things

still about a girl

are yours from me
and I'd give them again
and again and again
just so you wouldn't have to pretend anymore

why must we suffer alone

I want to tell you I understand
and how I think it true
that I am a man who truly can
know why you turned me away
to take all that I feel and all that I am

I'm sorry you have to do this alone
but there is no other way it can be
I suppose I just wish
and I suppose I just pray
that someday
me...you will need me

still about a girl

Sandy

she was here with me tonight
alone with me somewhere inside
fading away into love's light

outside 'neath the clouds of gray
Sandy had something to say
I didn't want to hear
she didn't want to be near it
but it was said anyway
she said, "You are what I've been trying to find
"in all my wasted time.
"And now that you're found,
"I don't want you around."

she says that she's breaking
so tired of waking....up
with no one home
she can't stand to be alone
and her sorrow is all I see
and, Sandy, you know
you don't have to go
you can take it slow
just please, please remember me
and she said, "You are who I want to sleep
"with in daydreaming flowers
"of what I'm trying to be,
"but it can't be you and me."

purple rain washes us away
in began to pour sometime yesterday
leading all that was astray
and Sandy walks away
can't you see all that I feel,
all that I know, all that is real?

or am I just a friend
who knows pain?
am I just a friend
who is the same
as you?

I'm so tired of being a nice guy
and led on through a string of lies
I'm sick of existing
as your telephone listing
the same as a dial tone

and she told me, "I thought of you as I laid awake,
"knowing that leaving was a mistake
"but I can't take no more
"of your care and all you adore."

Sandy thinks she doesn't deserve it
or how the wind blows of her song
she thinks that I don't understand it
and how all I feel is wrong

and I said I'm breaking
so tired of waking
with no one home
can't stand to be alone
and my sorrow is all she sees
and I know, I know
I have to go

my life is so damn slow
and she won't remember me

still about a girl

she gets it, you get it...I suppose I do, too

there is a rainbow
not of colors, but of black and white
blended together with gray
she sees me
she actually sees me
not as I am
but as I am
missing you, over and over

we talked tonight; my hand rested upon her knee
she seemed to understand, that part of her
just like you
just like me

behind her eyes I watch as her memory fades
her thoughts replaying the moment when life stopped
my life stopped
at the same time as hers; as yours
I wish things would start spinning again
but I hide, for I am not next in line
he first then he next
like a cycle

my turn will never come
my chance to forget you
I could never forget you
yet I may live
maybe not for tomorrow, maybe not for today
but for yesterday, yes, for yesterday

I am sick
my stomach is swirling like a pleasant night's sleep
something which kills this nightmare
and wakes me up

you're not there—no—yesterday

About the Author

A.P. Fuchs writes from Winnipeg, Manitoba. He is the author of several novels and short stories, nearly all of which have been published both in print and electronic form. Among his most recent are, *The Way of the Fog, Magic Man, A Red Dark Night,* and *April,* which was written under his pseudonym, Peter Fox. Visit him online at www.apfuchs.com

www.ingramcontent.com/pod-product-compliance
Lightning Source LLC
Chambersburg PA
CBHW021116080526
44587CB00010B/533